Electric Guitar

Simon Croft

HINKLER
BOOKS

This book is dedicated to guitar students everywhere

Project Manager/Editor: Kate Cuthbert
Head Design: Sam Grimmer
Design: Fiona Finn
Photography: Ned Meldrum

Special thanks to:
Chris Voce from Guitars Plus. www.guitarsplus.com.au
Stephen Miltchelmore, drums, and Davis Ross, bass,
for their assistance on the backing tracks.
Dave and Ross at Ulbrick Sound. www.ulbricksound.com.au

First published in 2008
by Hinkler Books Pty Ltd
45-55 Fairchild Street
Heatherton Victoria 3202 Australia
www.hinklerbooks.com.au

Printed and bound in China

HINKLER
BOOKS

ISBN 978 1 7418 2572 5

Contents

Introduction

One of the most popular instruments on the planet, the electric guitar is an instrument in its own right.

Some of the best music ever written and performed has been on the electric guitar and these works continue to be inspirational and timeless in their appeal. Works from artists such as The Beatles, Led Zeppelin, AC/DC, Queen, Jimi Hendrix and the Red Hot Chili Peppers appeal to audiences of all ages, and were all created on the electric guitar.

There is a popular misconception that students new to guitar should start with an acoustic instrument. Nothing could be further from the truth. While experience on the acoustic guitar may be a great asset, it is certainly not required to start learning electric guitar nor to be a great electric guitar player.

The purpose of this book is to pass on to you, the aspiring electric guitarist, as much practical information as possible, and, in doing so, set you off on the path to finding your own 'voice'.

The material covered will include detailed instructions on care of your instrument, a hardware section and some of the great playing techniques, all clearly explained with photos and easy to read diagrams, so you can learn at your own pace.

So grab your guitar and get ready. Let's tune up!

The Electric Guitar

Here's a diagram of a typical electric guitar. As you can see, there are quite a few parts involved, but, in time, you will remember the names of these parts – and what they do – without any trouble at all.

Choosing Your Guitar

Choosing your electric guitar can be a daunting task, but don't panic. There are many ways of finding (and understanding) the information you need to make an informed decision. For instance, your local guitar store employees are experts and it is their job to put the right instrument in your hands.

Here is a basic list of what you will need to get started:
1. An electric guitar
2. A small practice amplifier
3. A guitar lead
   (to connect the guitar
   to the amplifier)
4. A guitar strap
5. Some picks
   (sometimes referred
   to as plectrums)
6. An electronic guitar tuner
7. A guitar stand
8. Some spare guitar
   strings
9. A string winder
10. A metronome
11. A music stand

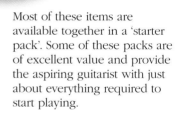

Most of these items are available together in a 'starter pack'. Some of these packs are of excellent value and provide the aspiring guitarist with just about everything required to start playing.

I strongly recommend for your first electric guitar that you get a model that features both types of picks-ups – a humbucker style pick up in the bridge position and two single coil pick-ups in the middle and neck position. The differences in these pick-ups are further discussed in the Getting the Right Sounds section.

Working parts of an Electric Guitar

1. Headstock
From here, you will tune your guitar.

2. Machine Heads
Machine heads are also called tuning pegs.

3. The Nut
At the end of the headstock is a small but important part of the guitar called the nut. The nut plays a big part in how well your guitar will play.

4. The Neck
The neck of the guitar joins the headstock and the body.

5. The Fingerboard and Frets
The front of the neck is called the fingerboard. The little metal bars that are mounted vertically on the fingerboard are called frets, and your left hand is what, from now on, we will call your fretting hand. The frets are numbered, starting from the head and going down to the body. So when a chord asks for the 5th fret, simply count down from the head until you reach five.

6. The Body
Moving down the neck, we come to the body. This is where the magic happens.

7. The Scratch Plate
The role of the scratch plate is to hold in the pick ups.

8. Pick Ups
Pick ups pick up the sound of the vibrating guitar strings, very much like a microphone amplifies the singing voice, and send these vibrations through to the guitar amplifier.

The pick up nearest the neck is called the 'neck pick up'. It gives a more mellow sound.

The middle pick up has a nice 'chiming' quality, almost like an acoustic guitar.

The pick up nearest the bridge is harsher, a good sound for a more aggressive tone.

9. Guitar Controls
You also have your volume and tone control switches. The most important control on your electric guitar is the volume control – this controls the amount of volume from your guitar to the amplifier.

The tone controls are generally set to full on your guitar. You have the best control of your tone from the amplifier, however, so feel free to experiment with these.

10. Input Jack
The input jack is where you'll plug in your guitar lead, or cable, and connect in to your amplifier.

11. Selector Switch
The selector switch allows you to change between pick-ups.

12. The Bridge
The bridge is responsible for keeping the guitar in tune. If you have problems keeping your guitar in tune, then a qualified and experienced guitar repairman may need to adjust the bridge accordingly.

Guitar Controls

Selector Switch

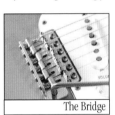
The Bridge

The Strings

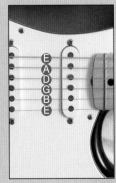

The strings are named from low E (thick), B, G, D, A and high E (thin).

Here's a handy saying to remember them:

Easter **B**unny **G**oes **D**ancing **A**t **E**aster

Open strings produce notes and sounds without any involvement from your fretting hand.

Connections

Once you've unpacked your instrument and accessories, the right connections between the equipment need to be made. It's always a good idea to read whatever instruction and technical manuals are provided with your purchase.

Here's a diagram of a basic practice set up:

Tuning

Getting (and keeping) your guitar in tune is one of the most important skills you can learn as a guitarist. Using an electric guitar tuner can help you tune up and start playing right away, however, it is an important skill to be able to tune a guitar by ear. This way you will be able to tell when your guitar needs tuning and fix it whenever and wherever you are.

Learning to tune a guitar the manual way – that is, without an electric tuner – is not easy at first, but over time, your ear will become attuned and it will become a lot easier.

Let's start with an electric tuner, so we can be sure your guitar is in tune.

What to do:
1. Plug your guitar lead into the tuner input marked 'in'. An easy way to remember this is that 'in' stands for 'instrument'.
2. Make sure the volume control of your guitar in turned all the way up. This allows the tuner to easily pick up the string vibration.
3. Tune your string so the tuning meter shows no movement.

Now let's tune manually.
1. Tune your A string using a tuner or a tuning fork. We'll start here because then your ear will, over time, start to recognise the sound of a correctly tuned note.

2. Place your first finger on the 5th fret on the A string. Play this note to produce a D note. Now, play the open D string and adjust the tuning peg until the notes sound the same. Do your best to make them as exact as possible.
3. Place your first finger on the 5th fret on the D string; play this note to produce a G note. Adjust the tuning peg of the open G string, remembering to get the two notes as close as possible.
4. Place your first finger on the 4th fret on the G string. This produces a B note. Play your open B string and tune until both notes sound exactly the same.
5. Place your first finger on the 5th fret on the B string; play this note to produce a E note. Adjust the tuning peg of the open E string until you produce the same note.
6. Use your open high E string to tune your low E string. These notes will be an octave apart, but you should be able to hear when they are the same.
7. Check your tuning with an electronic tuner if possible.

Caring for Your Instrument

When you're not playing your guitar, it should be stored in a safe place: on a stand or in its case. Extreme temperatures must be avoided, as excessive heat or cold can cause irreversible damage to your instrument.

I recommend keeping your guitar on a guitar stand; this way you'll be encouraged to pick it up and practise more often. When cleaning your guitar, always wipe down your strings with a dry lint-free cloth and do not use any cleaners other than recommended guitar-specific ones.

String Breakages

String breakages can happen to the best guitar players at the worst of times!

It's a good idea to learn how to do this yourself now as, like with playing your guitar, the more you do it, the better you will become.

Here's a quick reference to changing your broken string.

1. Remove all remnants of the broken string, taking care with the sharp ends.
2. Install new string and cut the end two tuning peg lengths past where you intend to wind it on.
3. Bend the string to lock it in.
4. Wind the first wrap under the string and use the string winder to wind the rest of the string on, taking care not to over wind. Keep the windings as neat as possible.
5. Clip the string close to the peg

It may take a couple of attempts, but you'll soon get the hang of changing a broken string.

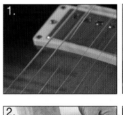

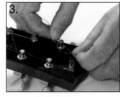

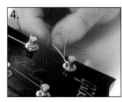

At the Beginning

Holding the Pick

Over the years I've taught a lot of students, and one common error that students make is assuming the fretting hand is more important than the picking hand. Nothing could be further from the truth. Both hands are equally important, and it's essential that you learn to hold the pick in a way that is comfortable for you to play both chords and scales.

Right handed players should rest the pick between the top right edge of the thumb and the top left side of the first finger of the right hand. Left handed players should use the same method, only in the left hand.

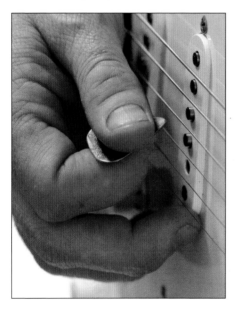

From this point forward, we will refer to the right hand as the pick hand, and the left as the fretting hand. Left handed players will need to remember to use the opposite.

The pick should be held firmly, but not cause excess tension in the forearm, elbow or shoulder.

Try not to show too much pick to the strings. This makes it a lot easier to control your sound.

Now strike the strings with your pick.

Try picking on the open D string, remembering the following tips:
1. Pick up and down always.
2. Speed is not important here, just accuracy.
3. Always use a metronome.

Tip: Up and down picking is used mainly for single note work, which is used when playing lead guitar. Playing only down strokes on the chords is okay, and is a rhythm guitar technique.

Let's practise by playing some open strings. Open strings are played without any interference from your fretting hand. Play each string – E, B, G, D, A and E – slowly, aiming for precision and clarity. Repeat this exercise until you're completely comfortable with your pick.

The Fretting Hand

Now is a good time to review the role of the fretting hand and introduce some new techniques and exercises for fretting and picking.

Pick and Fingers

The pick and fingers approach may be more identified with country music or acoustic guitar players, but it is a very valuable skill for aspiring guitar players of any style to develop.

This approach involves holding the pick as described earlier in the book, with one major difference. While you are using the pick to play the lower part of the chords (generally the E, A and D strings) you can use the 2nd and 3rd fingers of your picking hand to pick notes on the three higher strings, the G, B and E strings.

At first, this is probably going to feel very strange as far as the pick hand is concerned, like you are making a grab for the strings. You may find that the sound you produce at first is unbalanced. This is because, at this point in time, the pick is producing a louder sound than the softer picking fingers.

The reason for this is, as with the finger tips of your fretting hand when you first get started, the tips of the fingers on your picking hand are soft. They will also get quite sore. Should you wish to make the pick and fingers approach a part of your regular practice regime, in time the tips of these fingers will harden and you'll be able to work on this technique for a longer period. The sound will then become a lot more even.

This technique can be used for lead guitar also. It may come as a surprise, but all of the lead guitar work on the Dire Straits song *Sultans of Swing* is, in fact, played just using fingers!

3–4 Exercise

1. Place your first finger right behind the third fret, pick the note. Make sure the sound is clear.
2. Place your second finger behind the fourth fret and now pick this note. Do your best not to lift your first finger.

Now, a couple of important things you should remember: try and keep your fingers as close to the fret board as possible. This will certainly take some concentration. You can expand this warm up exercise to different combinations of your fretting hand: you can play the same exercise for fingers 1 and 2, fingers 2 and 3, fingers 3 and 4, fingers 1 and 3 on frets 3 and 5, then fingers 1 and 4 on frets 3 and 6.

Exercises like this are great for warming up every time you play. Remember, the guitar is a physical instrument and you have to be warmed up to play your best.
Take your time and your fingers will soon become accustomed to this technique.

Now let's try the same exercise with fingers 3 and 4.
1. Place your third finger right behind the third fret, pick the note. Make sure the sound is clear.
2. Now place your fourth finger behind the fourth fret and pick this note. Do your best not to lift your third finger.

You'll naturally find this harder but it's certainly going to be worth all the effort. I still do this exercise everyday and I've been playing many years.

Try to pick up and down at all times. Don't rush: we're after accuracy, not speed.

After some time playing, you may notice the tips of your fingers on your fretting hand getting sore. This is perfectly normal and, after a few weeks, your fingertips will harden and become calloused and you'll be able to play for longer periods of time.

The Importance of TAB

Let's look at TAB, which is also known as guitar tablature. TAB offers a graphic representation of the guitar using six lines (one for each guitar string) as opposed to the five lines used in traditional notation.

The use of TAB among guitar players is very popular for a number of reasons, but mostly because sight reading traditional notation for guitar can be very difficult. A guitar offers many different options for playing the same piece of music, where a piano, for instance, offers only one.

Let's look at the example of the 3–4 exercise you just played represented in the TAB format.

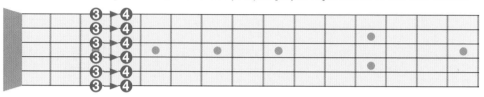

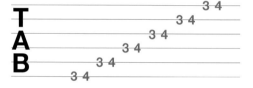

To read TAB the correct way, you must look at TAB as if you are looking over your guitar neck. There are six staff lines with TAB, one for each string – the lowest string, E, is the one nearest the bottom of the page and the highest string, E, is at the top of the page. The numbers on the lines of the TAB represent the fret numbers; read the TAB as with standard music notation, from left to right. 'Stacked' numbers represent a chord and exactly where it is to be played. Chords are also displayed with diagrams, which is like TAB, but rotated to show where your fingers should be placed. We'll use mostly diagrams through the book.

While TAB is considered the industry standard and is used in guitar magazines around the world to offer accurate transcriptions of popular guitar music, it should be noted that it does have its limitations. TAB does not provide an insight into the timing that standard notation does, so it's a good idea to try and use both in time. Finding a good music teacher will help you with reading and understanding music, or you can check out any of the number of books available on reading music.

Tip: When working with TAB, try to find familiar patterns within the transcription. It may be chords or scales within the tab that you've seen before. Recognising these patterns can save a lot of time when you're learning a song or piece of music.

Chords

Chords are notes played together. They give you, the guitarist, the ability to play by yourself or within a group.

While it won't be possible to show you all the chords in this book, I'll show you enough to get you on the right path. There are literally thousands of chords, so it may be a good idea to get a chord dictionary from your local guitar store, and get a good teacher as soon as possible.

It is a good idea to learn the chords by name and shape – that way you'll have more than one way to remember the chords. Chords are named after the first note of the chord.

Use only down strokes (strums) with the pick and make sure you are only hitting the strings you need to, otherwise the chord sound may become muddled.

Since the typical electric guitar player is playing rhythm guitar about 98% of the time (usually within a group of four or five players and to complement vocals), it is very important that you learn these essential chords.

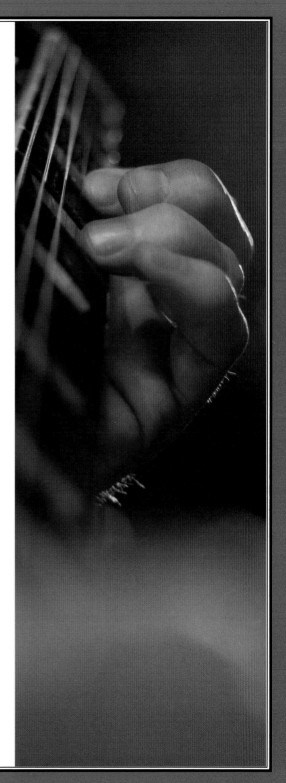

Open Chords

Let's try the open chords of E, D and A. These are called open chords because they rely on the sound of an open string for their sound. You'll probably remember that an open string is played without any interference from your fretting hand.

Your fingers should look like they are growing out of the finger board.

E

D

A

A 2

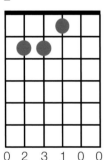

0 2 3 1 0 0

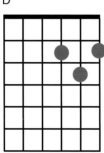

X X 0 1 3 2

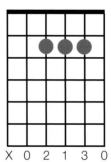

X 0 2 1 3 0

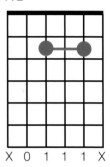

X 0 1 1 1 X

To play an E chord:
1. Place your first finger just behind the first fret on the G string.
2. Now place your second finger just behind the second fret on the A string.
3. To complete the finger placement of this chord, place your third finger just behind the second fret on the D string.
4. All the remaining strings are open: the low E string, the B string and the high E string – meaning no fingers are placed on them.
5. Play all six strings.

To play a D chord:
1. Place your first finger just behind the second fret on the G string.
2. Place your second finger just behind the second fret on the high E string.
3. Place your third finger behind the third fret on the B string.
4. Play this chord from the open D string, avoiding the low E and the A strings.

To play an A chord, traditionally:
1. Place your first finger behind the second fret on the G string.
2. Place your second finger behind the second fret on the D string.
3. Place your third finger behind the second fret of the B string.
4. Play this chord from the open A string and include the open high E string, but not the low E string.

Alternatavely:
The second way to play the A chord is to use just the first finger to play the notes on the D, B and G strings at the second fret. For this particular chord fingering, we again play from the A string. However, this time, we don't include either E string.
   This chord fingering is very useful as it liberates your second and third fingers, which you can then use to expand on this chord. There are a lot of songs that have just three chords, even the three chords we've just learned.

Essential Chords

These chords are the most common of guitar chords, so it's a great idea to commit them to memory as soon as you can. I find learning them in pairs works really well, as you'll be able to work at chord changing at the same time. Chord changing will be covered in more detail in the More Advanced Chords and Scales section of this book, but you can start trying to change between them now.

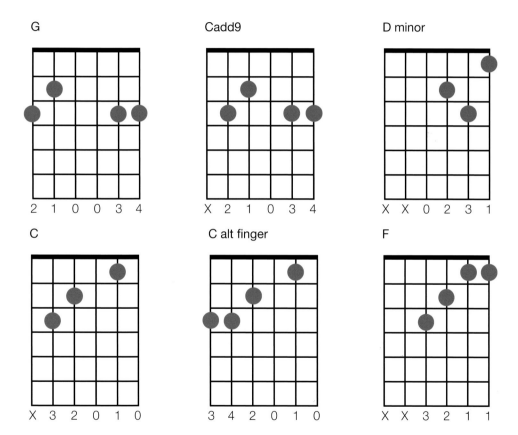

| G | Cadd9 | D minor |
| C | C alt finger | F |

Tips:

1. At this stage it's a good idea for you to practise with a clean sound – no distortion, overdrive or effects. This way you'll be able to hear how you're playing a lot more clearly.
2. Review all chord shapes as often as possible. Your fingers will start to remember the shapes a lot quicker, making changing between chords much easier.

Essential Chords

D7

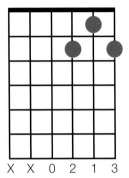

X X 0 2 1 3

G7

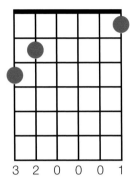

3 2 0 0 0 1

C7

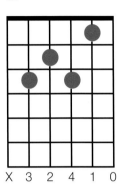

X 3 2 4 1 0

B7

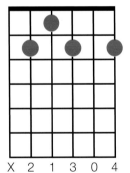

X 2 1 3 0 4

G minor

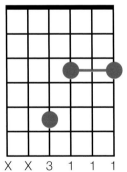

X X 3 1 1 1

F minor

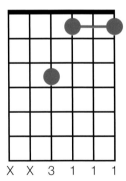

X X 3 1 1 1

Tips:
1. Try and remember the chords in pairs, so you'll have more practice at changing between chords.
2. Don't be afraid to experiment with different strumming patterns. Try to emulate drum beats in your strumming pattern to give your playing a more percussive feel.

Essential Scales

As with chords, scales are a very essential element of good electric guitar playing. We'll look at the scales you'll need to navigate your way around the guitar neck.

Fret Notes on Guitar

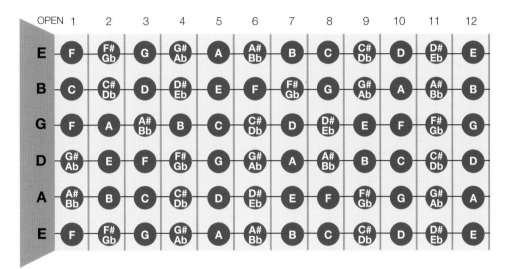

This diagram displays all the notes on the guitar neck up to the 12th Fret. If this is new to you, it will look like a confusing mass of notes. Don't panic! There is a discernable pattern that will become obvious in a short amount of time.

Tips:
1. Learn one string a week.
2. Look for patterns. You'll find the notes always run in the same sequence: A# always follows A, regardless of which string you're playing on. Using patterns will help you become more familiar with the order of notes and how they appear on the guitar neck.

The Major Scale

Scales are a sequence of single notes constructed to a formula to establish a specific melodic sequence. Sound confusing? It does not have to be. Simply put, scales are your musical alphabet.

The major scale is the most important scale in music, although, in the electric guitar, its use is not as common as in other instruments. However, it makes sense to have a solid knowledge of this scale, as every scale in Western music uses it.

Also, it should be noted that all other scales, including the scales you will learn later on in the book, are an altered form of the major scale. Although you may not need or use this information right away, having a working knowledge of the major scale will be invaluable later.

The scale is named after the note you start the scale from, sometimes referred to as the 'tonic', 'key' or 'root' note.

Let's focus first on the C major scale. The notes for this scale are C D E F G A B C. This pattern is exactly the same for all other major scales. Start with the key, or tonic, note – that

is, the note the scale is named after – and play the 8 notes in sequence. This is a great way to learn the notes on the guitar neck as well.

Try to play both slowly and smoothly.

To play a C Major scale:
1. Place your second finger on the third fret on the A string, pick this note.
2. Place your fourth finger on the fifth fret on the A string and pick this note.
3. Place your first finger at the second fret on the D string, play this note.
4. Place your second finger on the third fret at the D string, play this note.
5. Place your fourth finger at the fifth fret on the D string and pick this note.
6. Move your first finger to the second fret on the G string and play this note.
7. Move your third finger to the fourth fret on the G string, play this note.
8. Move your fourth finger to the fifth fret on G string.

You've just learned the notes C D E F G A B C – the C major scale. Here's how this scale appears on the neck and TAB:

C Major Scale

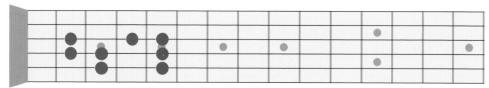

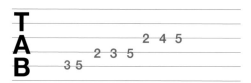

fingers   2   4   1   2   4   1   3   4

Tips:

1. Try to keep your fingers as close to the guitar neck as possible, like the picture above.

2. Always try to use up and down pick strokes. This will help you play this scale (or any other scale) faster as you become more comfortable with the pattern.

3. After practising this scale for some time, your fingers will start to memorise this scale by how it feels. This is known as

muscle memory and can be a very valuable tool for learning (and remembering) patterns, notes and chords.

4. As with chords, play these notes with the tips of your fingers. Unfortunately, you may experience some soreness when you first start to play, but this will settle down after a little while.

5. Scales are a great way to warm up when starting a

G Major Scale

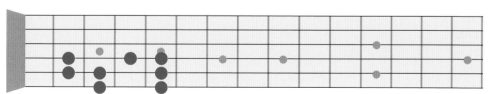

Moveable Scales

The major scales are examples of moveable scales, which means that they can be played at many different locations on the guitar neck.

For example, let's consider the note of A. When you play the A Major scale, you have to start with A. However, the A note appears in many different places on the guitar neck. So once you learn the shapes of these scales, you can play them wherever you want on the neck, in every different key – which means at a higher or lower pitch.

A moveable scale shape involves no open strings. Once you learn the shape for the A Major scale, you can move it to the fifth fret

on the low E string, where the A note is. Play the same shape and you have the A Major scale.

So by using the moveable major scale shape, we can learn the major scale in all keys and, at the same time, learn all the notes on the guitar neck.

I think it's a great idea to make playing the major scale a part of your daily practice routine.

A Major Scale

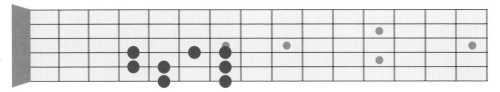

fingers   2   4   1   2   4   1   3   4

Pentatonic Minor Scales

The Pentatonic scale is the most widely used scale in rock and popular music. Pentatonic is Latin for 'five tones', which means that this scale has only five notes. Let's look at the most common fingering for this scale on this diagram.

Pentatonic A Minor Scale

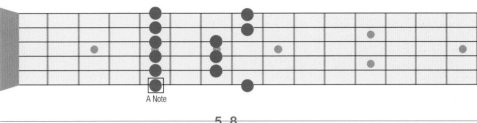

A Note

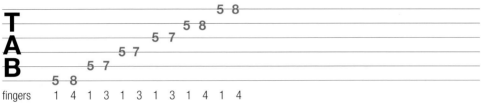

fingers   1   4   1   3   1   3   1   3   1   4   1   4

1. Your first finger plays the fifth fret on the low E string.
2. Your fourth finger plays the eighth fret on the low E string.
3. Moving up to the A string, play the fifth fret with the first finger.
4. Still on the A string, play the seventh fret with your third finger.
5. On the D string, your first finger plays the fifth fret.
6. On the D string, your third finger plays the seventh fret.
7. You should be seeing the pattern now: on the G string, your first finger plays the fifth fret.
8. Still on the G string, your third finger plays the seventh fret.
9. On the B string, your first finger plays the fifth fret.
10. On the B string, your fourth finger plays the eighth fret.
11. On the high E string, your first finger goes to the fifth fret.
12. On the high E string, your fourth finger plays the eighth fret.

You have just played the notes A C D E G A C D E G A C – or the Pentatonic A Minor scale twice through. You'll notice that this pattern is almost box-shaped; it is sometimes referred to as the 'box position'.

There are five different patterns for the Pentatonic Scale in each key. The example above is the first pattern. We'll cover the others more thoroughly later in the book.

Memorise this scale, as you'll find yourself using it quite extensively as you become more confident.

More Advanced Chords and Scales

To be a good rhythm guitar player, you'll need a solid knowledge of chords and the ability to change chords smoothly and cleanly. You will also need to have a solid sense of timing and dynamics, by which I mean you'll need to know when to play loudly or softly or sometimes, even, not at all.

To be a good lead guitarist, you will need to know all the notes on the low E string and have a thorough knowledge of the Pentatonic Minor scale and the Major scale. You'll also need to be able to match a scale to a chord sequence so that your solo playing will stay in key.

Being able to play both rhythm and lead guitar makes a great guitar player!

This can be achieved by you!

Let's get started.

Changing Chords

Changing chords is one of the biggest challenges that every guitar student faces.

Tips:
1. Learn chords in pairs, for example, A minor and C.
2. Look for common fingerings. With A minor and C, the first and second finger play the same note on either chord, so work on moving only the fingers you need to. For these chords, moving only the third finger will take you from the A minor to the C chord.
3. Repetition and patience are the keys to chord changing success.

Bar Chords and Power Chords

Now, it's time for us to move onto bar chords and power chords. The bad news is that these chords are a little harder to play than the open chords, but there is good news and that is there are less shapes to learn.

The E Chords
A bar chord is named because your fingers create a 'bar' across the strings. These chords are moveable shapes, which means you can play them at many different places on the neck of the guitar. Based on two open shapes that we've seen before, you can play the open E chord like I showed you in the At The Beginning chapter, but you can also play the E chord with these fingers.

The altered fingering for the altered E chord shape is as follows:
1. Your second finger holds down the G string on the second fret.
2. Your third finger holds down the second fret on the A string.
3. Your fourth finger holds down the note on the second fret on the D string.

Now you have freed up your first finger, so move this shape up one fret and place your first finger over all six strings at the first fret. This chord is named F major as we have moved the chord to F which is the note at the first fret on the E string.

F Major

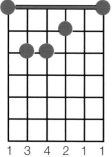

1 3 4 2 1 1

Once you have this chord in place it is only a matter of changing the fingering very slightly to play the minor, the seventh and the minor seventh chords. The important thing to remember is that your first finger will always cover all six strings for the set of bar chords based on the E chords.

Once again, the importance of learning and remembering the notes on the low E string will come into play here. You'll also now need to learn the notes on the A string. This is because there are two sets of bar/power chords.

Minor Chord
We can change this chord to a minor chord by removing your second finger from the G string.

F Minor

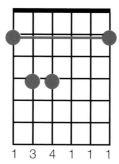

1 3 4 1 1 1

Remember, your first finger is still covering all six strings and your third and fourth fingers stay in the same place: on the second fret of the A string and the second fret on the D string.

If we move this up to the third fret, we name it after the note on the low E string at the third fret which is a G – now we have a G minor chord.

Minor chords have a distinctly different sound from the major: they are more sad and dramatic.

7th Chord

I would now like to introduce you to the seventh chord (7th). It is close in sound to the major chord but different in a subtle way.

F 7th

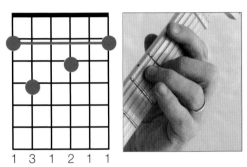

1 3 1 2 1 1

The 7th chord has an almost bluesy quality; it is used in jazz and blues guitar styles, but was also used by the Beatles in a lot of their compositions.

The F7 Chord:
1. Place your first finger over all strings at the first fret.
2. Your second finger plays the second fret on the G string.
3. Your third finger plays the third fret on the A string.

We can also play a seventh chord by fingering the major chord and removing your fourth finger. I'll remind you again that your first finger at this stage should be covering all six strings.

To change this to other 7th chords, simply move the shape along the neck. Where your first finger falls determines which 7th chord you're playing.

Minor 7th Chord

We can now learn the final bar chord based on the E shape and that will bring us to the minor seventh (m7) chord.

F Minor 7th

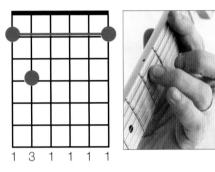

1 3 1 1 1 1

Let's now play an Fm7 chord; the fingering for this is:
1. First finger holds down all six strings at the first fret.
2. Third finger plays the second fret on the A string.

The minor seventh chord is used a lot in Latin influenced rock such as Santana.

The A Chords
The second set of bar chords is based on the open A chord.

It is extremely useful to know both sets of chords: if you only knew the E based bar chords, you would be working much harder than you need to. For example, if you needed to play G minor to C minor and you only knew the E based bar chords, you would be playing a chord on the third fret and then moving up the neck to play the C minor (Cm) at the eighth fret!

If you know your fifth string – or A – bar chords, you will know that the Cm based on the fifth string (A shape) is at the third fret, much more efficient.

Let's look at learning the A based bar chords.

Major Chord
This is based on the A shape we learned earlier. Before, the notes on the second fret on the D, G and B strings were held down by your first finger.

Bb Major

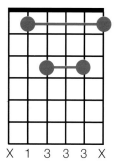

X 1 3 3 3 X

For this chord:
1. Use your third finger to hold down the second fret on the D, G and B strings.

2. Move your third finger up one fret to the third fret.
3. Once again you have freed up your first finger.
4. Place your first finger on the first fret on the A string, this note is a B flat or Bb.
5. Play all the strings except the Low E and the high E strings.

Remember, these sets of chords will be named by the corresponding notes on the A string, always played by your first finger.

Minor Chord
Lets look at the minor chord based on the A shape.

C Minor

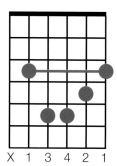

X 1 3 4 2 1

For a C minor (Cm) chord:
1. Place your first finger across the third fret from the A string, so you are covering five strings.
2. Place your second finger on the fourth fret on the B string.
3. Your third finger will be playing the fifth fret on the D string.
4. Your fourth finger will be playing the fifth fret on the G string.

To play the A based minor seventh chord, just remove your fourth finger from the previous fingering.

7th Chord

To play an A based 7th chord, let's look at a D7 chord for example. Remember, the note on the fifth fret A string is a D.

D7

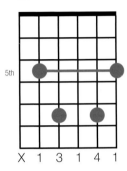

X   1   3   1   4   1

1. Place your first finger across the A, D, G, B and High E strings at the fifth fret. We don't need Low E for these chords.
2. As the chord here is named after the note on the fifth string, your third finger plays the seventh fret on the D string.
3. Your fourth finger plays the seventh fret on the B string.

Now the even better news: once you've mastered these chords, you have the power chords covered!

Power chords are used in many styles of guitar playing, such as rock, heavy metal, punk rock and pop. These power chords are also referred to as 5th chords.

To play the power chords, or 'fifth' chords, you only have to sound the first two strings of the chords.

Now I know these chords are physically harder to play, so take your time and make sure you take regular breaks. However, the sooner you become more comfortable with these chords, the sooner you'll be able to play more music and more songs.

The 12 Bar Blues Pattern

The 12 bar blues pattern is possibly the most commonly used chord progression in blues music and blues-influenced rock music. With this in mind, it's a good idea to look at this pattern in some detail.

The 12 bar blues pattern is simply 12 bars of music played, then repeated. We'll look at an example in the key of E, then at developing a slightly different style of playing the rhythm pattern. These are all variations of chords that you already know.

The 12 bar chord progression is known as a I, IV, V progression, or, to use our numbers, a 1, 4, 5 chord progression. This simply means that the chords are taken from the first, fourth and fifth notes of their corresponding major scale.

For example, to get the chords for a 12 bar progression in E, simply list the notes in the E major scale: E, F#,G# A, B, C#, D#, E (octave). 1 = E, 4 = A and 5 = B. These are your chords for a 12 bar progression in the key of E.

If you decide that you want to play this progression in another key, for example A, then list the notes of the A major scale: A, B, C#, D, E, F#,G#, A (octave).1 = A, 4 = D, 5 = E. You have now changed key and worked out the 3 chords required to play a 12 bar blues progression in the key of A.

If you use the method above, you can work out the chords for a 12 bar blues progression in any key.

You'll notice that the E and A chords we are using are being played mainly on two strings. This is very common in rock and blues music and is a very effective way of playing a professional sounding chord progression.

If you want to work out the chords for a twelve bar in the key of G, then this time use the first, fourth and fifth notes from the G major scale. For now, though we'll stay in the key of E. Now, let's try the following example.

Here's how to play the first four bars, which I'll call the 'E' section.

What you do:
1. Place your first finger at the second fret on the A string and play this together with the open low E string twice.
2. Straight after that, place your third finger at the fourth fret on the A string and play this twice along with the open low E string.
3. Move your fourth finger to the fifth fret on the A string and play this along with the open low E string twice.
4. Finally, once again play the note on the fourth fret on the A string along with the low open E string.
5. Repeat this process four times in total and you have the first four bars of a twelve bar blues pattern in the key of E.

The next two bars, which we will call the 'A' section, are the same, only this time we play the corresponding notes on the D string along with the open A string.

What you do:
1. Place your first finger at the second fret on the D string and play this together with the open A string twice.
2. Straight after that place your third finger at the fourth finger on the D string and play this twice along with the open A string.
3. Move your fourth finger to the fifth fret on the D string and play this along with the open A string twice.

4. Finally, once again play the note on the fourth fret on the D string along with the open A string.
5. Play this section twice and then return to the first four bars, only this time you play the section for only two bars.

And of course, the final four.

For one bar, play the B7 chord as noted in the TAB, then play one bar of the 'A' section once again.

What to do:
1. Place your first finger at the second fret on the D string and play this together with the open A string twice.
2. Place your third finger at the fourth fret on the D string and play this twice along with the open A string.
3. Move your fourth finger to the fifth fret on the D string and play this along with the open A string twice.
4. Finally, once again play the note on the fourth fret on the D string along with the open A string.

Follow this by one bar of the 'E' section.

What to do:
1. Place your first finger at the second fret on the A string and play this together with the open low E string twice.
2. Place your third finger at the fourth fret on the A string and play this twice along with the open low E string.
3. Move your fourth finger to the fifth fret on the A string and play this along with the open low E string twice.
4. Finally, once again play the note on the fourth fret on the A string along with the low open E string.

Play one bar of the 'A' section, and finish with four down strums of the B7 chord as noted in the TAB.

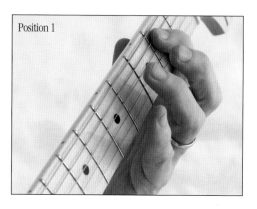

Position 1

There's a nice contrast if you play the B7 chord as a fuller sounding chord than the 'E' and the 'A' sections.

There you have the twelve bars.

If you study the above diagrams, you will see that by anchoring your first finger at the 2nd fret and using your 3rd finger to play the 4th fret and your 4th finger to play the note at the 5th fret, your 2nd, 4th & 5th fingers are playing different notes on the same string.

You can use this technique to play both the E and A chord sections of the 12 bar pattern.

As you become more confident with this piece, it will be a good idea to practise at many different tempos, as this style of playing has been used in many tempos across many different songs.

Tip: A good way to add variation to a 12 bar blues chord progression is to substitute some or all of the chords for their corresponding seventh chords.

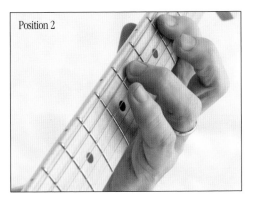

Position 2

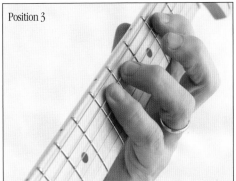

Position 3

%
means
repeat

12 Bar Blues

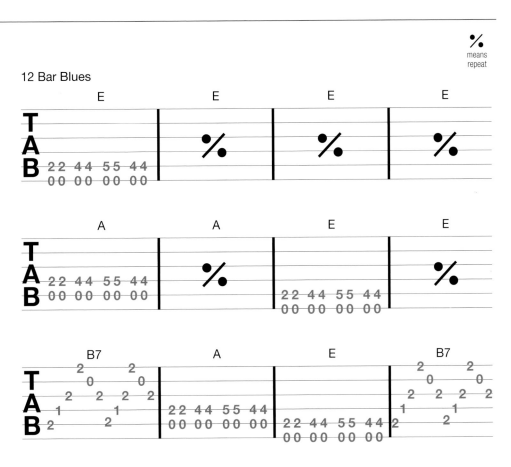

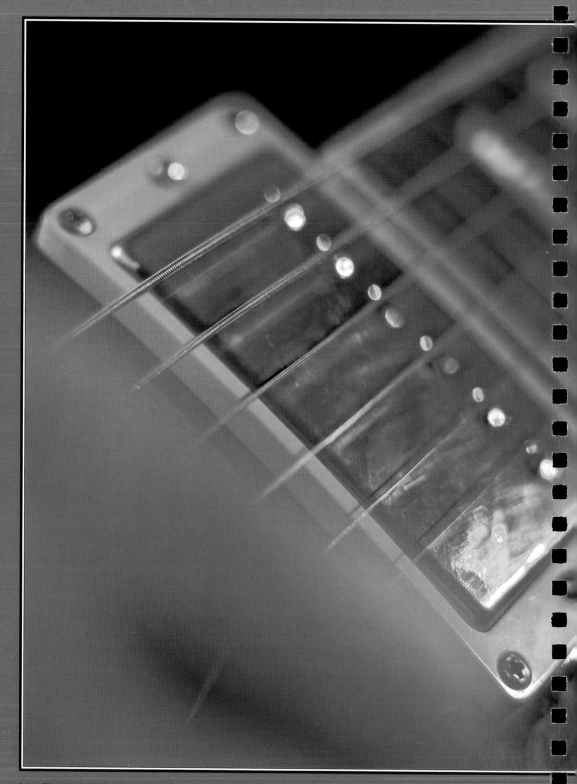

12 Bar Variations

There are many variations of the 12 bar blues pattern, and we certainly won't be able to cover them all here. However, we'll study one more example to give you a solid grounding in this style so you will be well prepared to study or research this style of music further, should you wish to do so.

Let's keep the following example in E. This is commonly know as a 'minor blues'. Notice how the 12 bar chord sequence takes on a totally different sound and feel.

By studying and playing the 12 bar examples in this section of the book, you'll be well prepared to continue studying this style of play.

%
means
repeat

12 Bar Variation

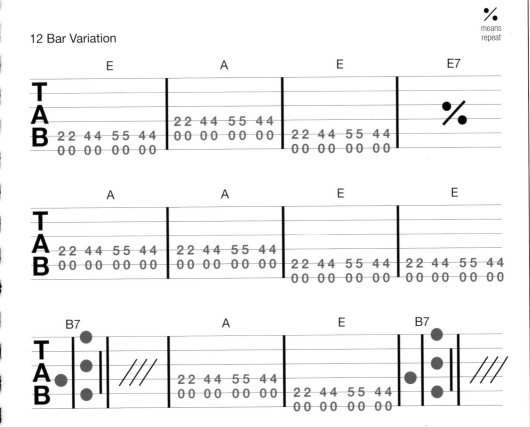

All Five Pentatonic Shapes

Up to now we have been using just the one Pentatonic Minor scale, however there are 5 patterns to learn. They can all be used together and they are all moveable, just like bar chords and power chords, so they can be used in all keys.

This may seem like a lot to learn, but let's check out these diagrams and TAB examples.

All 5 pentatonic minor scale positions

Position 1

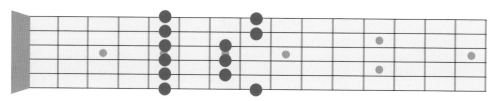

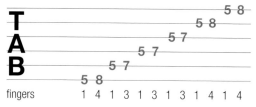

Position 2

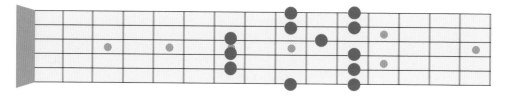

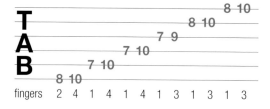

Tips:
1. Give yourself one week on each shape and learn it thoroughly.
2. Learn the shapes directly next to the one you've just learned and try to link these shapes in your head and with your fingers.
3. There is no right or wrong way to play between these shapes, just wrong notes! However, try to learn the fingerings covered on the scales before experimenting with your own fingerings; after some time you will find out what works best for you.

Position 3

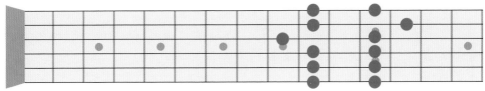

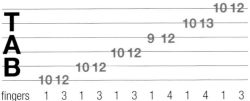

fingers   1   3   1   3   1   3   1   4   1   4   1   3

Position 4

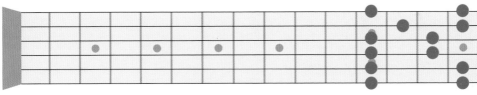

fingers   1   4   1   4   1   3   1   3   1   4   1   4

Position 5

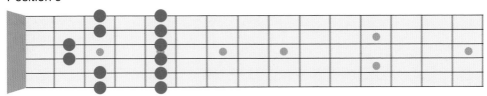

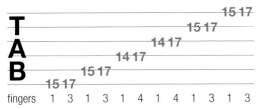

fingers   1   3   1   3   1   4   1   4   1   3   1   3

Ok, let's take a break. There is a lot of information to absorb here, so be sure to take your time and don't rush. If you can, make some large diagrams of the guitar neck, map out the shapes as they appear on the guitar fingerboard and put them up on the wall next to your bed. Spend about five or ten minutes studying these diagrams before you go to sleep: this is a really effective way of remembering and linking these pentatonic shapes in your head.

The Blues Scale

This scale is very similar to the Pentatonic Minor scale in appearance, however it has 6 tones instead of 5.

Blues Scale

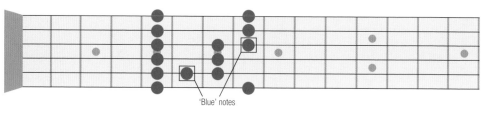

'Blue' notes

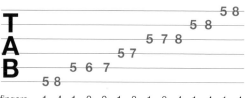

fingers   1   4   1   2   3   1   3   1   3   4   1   4   1   4

The extra note truly adds an extra flavour to the Pentatonic Minor scale. It is important to note that just because this scale is called the blues scale does not mean it can be only used when playing the blues. This scale can be heard in jazz, hard rock and heavy metal music.

The blues scale is one of my favourites, as it has a great sound, especially when used with the Pentatonic Minor scale.

The Natural Minor Scale

This scale could be considered the full version of the Pentatonic Minor scale. When used correctly, this scale has a very mysterious sound, moody, almost melancholy. This scale can be heard in the works of Carlos Santana.

Natural Minor Scale

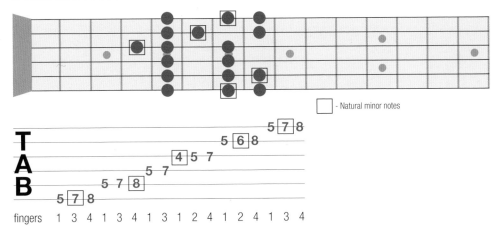

□ - Natural minor notes

```
        5 7 8
      5 6 8
T     4 5 7
A   5 7
B 5 7 8
  5 7 8
```

fingers   1 3 4 1 3 4 1 3 1 2 4 1 2 4 1 3 4

Try this chord progression for the A natural minor scale:

Natural Minor Chord Progression

```
        Am              G              F              Em
T   0           3              1              0
    1           3              1              0
A   2           0              2              0
    2           0              3              2
B   0           2              X              2
                3              X              0
```

Tips:

1. When you improvise with a scale, remember, you don't have to use all the notes in the scale. Look for the melody first.

2. Rather than trying to impress your listeners with how many scales you know, sometimes it's a good strategy just to play and see what comes out. If you like the sound of what you are playing, chances are you are on the right track. You may surprise yourself.

3. Review all the scales on a regular basis. This way, when you work on your scales, your playing will evolve and not sound like someone just running up and down the same scales.

4. Listen to your favourite guitar player often. You'll be able to hear how he or she uses the scales that you are playing to develop a lead guitar vocabulary.

Getting the Right Sounds

Playing Techniques

Accents

This is an important subject often overlooked by guitar students. An accent is simply highlighting a part in the music, usually by playing this part quite a bit louder. The correct use of accents can make even the most simple of chord progressions sound very effective.

Let's try this on some of the chords you have already learned, but with these simple accents.

String Damping or Muting

The technique known as muting or damping is a method of controlling the tone of the strings. You can make your chords or scales sound a little heavier or 'chunky' by resting the heel of your right hand against the strings where the bridge is on your guitar.

```
          V                                                    V = accents
     2   2   2   2           2   2   2   2
T    3   3   3   3           3   3   3   3
A    2   2   2   2           2   2   2   2
     0   0   0   0           0   0   0   0
B
     ⊓   ⊓   ⊓   ⊓           ⊓   ⊓   ⊓   ⊓
```

Palm Mute Throughout

This technique takes a little while to get the hang of as it restricts the movement of your picking hand slightly. Be careful not to over-mute the sound of the strings or you'll mask the overall character of the chords.

If you use this technique in addition to the accents, you'll have another rhythm technique to make the same simple chord sequences sound even more effective.

Heavy and Light Chords

Let's look at a couple of different playing approaches to the same chords. It's very rare that an electric guitar player playing a chord progression will play all of the strings all of the time. Why? Because you simply do not need to!

If you were to play all the strings all of the time, then your guitar playing style would sound repetitive and uninteresting. We can look at developing guitar parts within a group or ensemble situation, much like a simplified orchestra.

Let's look at the following short chord progression.

In the first example, we will opt for the heavier sounding chord inversions. These chords are played using the chord damping approach, so as to complement the first guitar part.

Heavy Chord Charts for Em, G, D, A

```
              V   Em   V                    G            V     D      V
                                      3                     2        2
 T                                    3                     3        3
 A                                    0                     2        2
 A   2 2 2 2 2 2 2 2                  0                0 0 0 0   0 0 0 0
 B   2 2 2 2 2 2 2 2                  2
     0 0 0 0 0 0 0 0                  3 3 3 3 3 3 3 3
     ⊓ ⊓ ⊓ ⊓ ⊓ ⊓ ⊓ ⊓
```

```
                 A
 T
 A
 A   2 2 2 2  2 2 2 2
 B   0 0 0 0  0 0 0 0
```

The second option is playing chords in a lighter fashion – that is, we'll pick certain strings from each chord and put it together like this:

```
         Em              G              D              A
          7               7              5              5
 T        8               8              7              5
 A        9               7              7              6
 A
 B
```

The lighter chords:

Em light
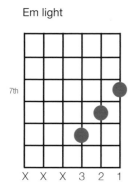
7th
X X X 3 2 1

G light
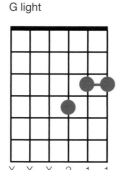
X X X 2 1 1

C light
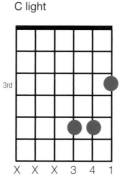
3rd
X X X 3 4 1

D light
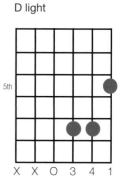
5th
X X O 3 4 1

G light
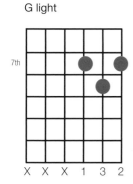
7th
X X X 1 3 2

Am7 light
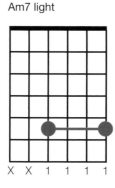
X X 1 1 1 1

A7 light
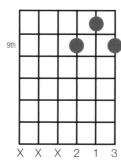
9th
X X X 2 1 3

Dm7 light
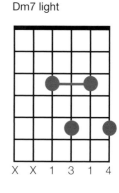
X X 1 3 1 4

Tips:
1. When you are working on guitar parts like this with other guitar players, it always makes good sense not to play too loud. You'll be able to hear what the other player is doing and you'll be able to lock into a groove far easier.
2. Make sure you try both ways of playing the same guitar part. You may find you are more confident and comfortable with the opposite part to which you were playing.

Dm11 light
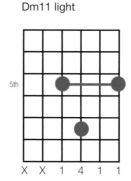
5th
X X 1 4 1 1

F▲7 light
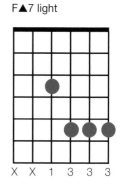
X X 1 3 3 3

The Hammer-on

The hammer-on is a technique where you pick only the first note and 'hammer on' to the next (higher) note. This technique is done by using the strength of your fretting hand to make the sound of the note(s) following the note played with a pick. This technique is almost like pushing into (but not bending to) the next note without picking it. In theory, you can sound many notes after the initial picked one, but it will depend on the strength of your picking hand, and will take a lot of practice to perfect.

The hammer-on as it appears on the neck and in TAB:

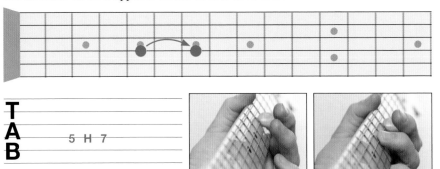

The Pull-off

The pull-off is essentially the opposite of the hammer-on, only this time you 'pull off' to a lower note. For example, play the 7th fret on the D string with your third finger. Also place your first finger on the 5th fret of the D string, so you have a note to pull off to. Play the first note, which is the 7th fret D string, and pull off by lifting your third finger, almost a flicking motion, to the note on the 5th fret D string.

The pull-off as it appears on the neck and in TAB:

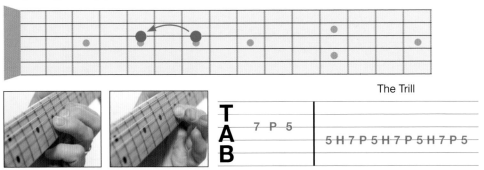

Combining Hammer-Ons And Pull-Offs
Combining the hammer-on and pull-off is a great way to make an effective lead solo or riff. This technique is sometimes referred to as a 'trill'.

Bending

Bending notes is an essential technique to master: you use it to change the pitch of one note to the next note in the scale. It does take a lot of effort to get the hang of this; try and get as many as your fingers under the string as you can.

Let's look at bending within the A pentatonic minor scale.

To bend, you need to have the pitch that you're aiming for in your mind. For example, play the note on the 7th fret G string; this is note you are bending from. Now play the note on the 9th fret G string, this is the pitch of the note you want to bend to. Use your third finger to bend, but have your first and second fingers ready to assist, by pushing the string up until you reach the same note as you would hear if you played the 9th fret on G.

This is how bending looks on TAB:

Bending takes a great deal of work! Don't get discouraged or frustrated right away.

Vibrato

While you're working on bending you should consider working on your vibrato; vibrato is the gradual release and restatement of a bend . It is hard to describe in words, but it's like a smooth waver in the pitch of the note; move the string up and down around the note you are playing.

This is how vibrato looks on TAB:

This is a great way to add expression and emotion to your playing. As with bending, it will take a lot of work to perfect.

I try to get my wrist and as many of my fingers involved as I can.

Sliding

Sliding is somewhat overlooked, I feel, but it's a very valid approach. Sliding adds some great personality to guitar playing. Instead of bending a note, you are shifting to the actual location of the note. You may find this easier than bending because you can use this on the heavier strings that are traditionally not bent.

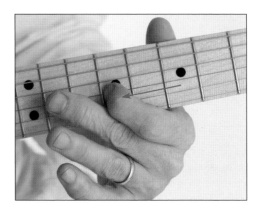

To slide, pick a note and really hold it down. Now try moving just to the next note either up or down in pitch. The sound you are aiming for should be smooth and seamless.
As you get more confident with this technique, try notes that are further apart.

Sliding is also a great way to add some great dimensions to your playing.

This is what sliding looks like on TAB:

Ghost Bend

Now I would like to touch on what I feel is one of the most effective lead guitar techniques. This is the ghost bend, sometimes referred to as the pre-bend. To do this, you need to bend a note accurately to pitch before you play it, so bend the note on the 7th fret G string, as we did previously in the first bending example, and then play it.

This is how a ghost bend appears on TAB:

This technique requires you to bend a note to the next pitch before you play it! It's difficult, but it sounds very effective.

I'm bending to the note that I'll play next.

This is a great way to start or finish a guitar solo.

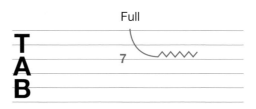

Pickup Selection

Your guitar will most likely have either two or three pick ups.

If you have a guitar with three single coil pick ups, then it most likely will have a 5-Way switch. This gives the guitar a wide variety of sounds that range from a harsher tone, using the bridge pick up, to a clean, 'glassy' tone, using the neck pick up.

This pick-up can also be used to get a sound close to that associated with the Red Hot Chili Peppers – a clean, bright, funky sound.

There are many tones in the 'out of phase' positions – achieved by placing the pick up selector in between the main pick ups (bridge, middle and neck).

Should you have a guitar with a humbucker pick up and two single coils pick-ups, then you will have louder, fuller sounding bridge pick ups with the versatility of having the sounds available using the two single coil pick ups. Another way of looking at this pickup arrangement is to view the humbucker as twice as powerful as the single coil pick up – after all, it is twice the size.

If you are the owner of guitar with two humbucker pick ups, don't worry! You will still have an array of different guitar tones at your disposal. The bridge position of a two humbucker pick up guitar will provide you with a big, rock style, 'crunch' sound, and the neck position pick up will give a rich, full, almost 'creamy' guitar tone, similar to guitar players like Carlos Santana and the early work of Eric Clapton.

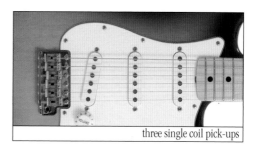

three single coil pick-ups

two single coil pick-ups and a humbucker pick-up

two humbucker pick-ups

The middle position of a dual Humbucker guitar can be used to emulate the twang of a single coil guitar tone.

Also, with the correct amplifier settings you can obtain a very distinctive sound by adjusting the tone control on your guitar, especially if you turn off the tone totally. By adjusting the tone knob to 0, you'll get something very close to the classic tone that identified Eric Clapton in his early guitar playing career.

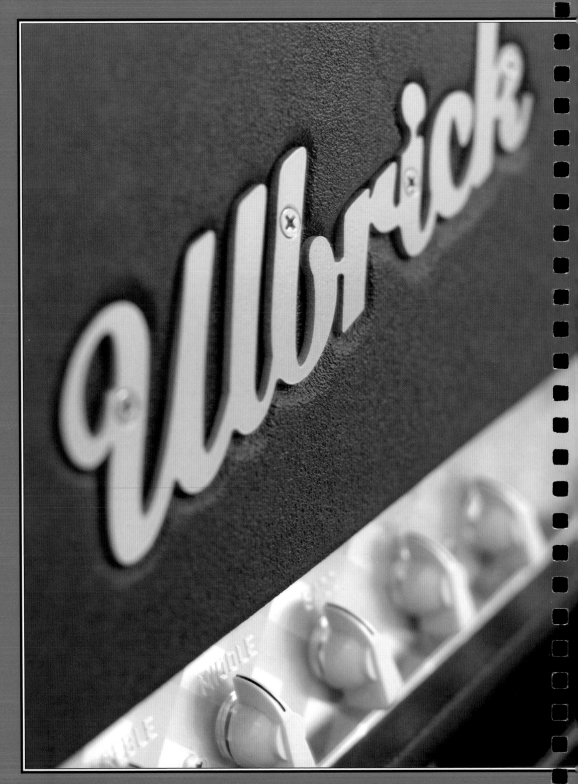

Adjusting the Guitar Amplifier

Every aspiring guitarist should learn how to use and adjust a guitar amplifier. If you are getting a really good guitar sound, then it is going to be more fun playing and practising.

Your sound is like your fingerprint, and you'll want to make a good impression whether you are playing in front of family, friends or fans.

In this section of the book, we'll look at some settings that you can apply even to the most basic in guitar gear, and get the sound you're looking for.

Your first guitar amp will most likely be a small practice style, but we'll also look a little at setting up bigger amps.

To set up your amp:
1. Set the master volume at the lowest possible setting and adjust the 'gain' or 'crunch' control gradually to decide which sound best suits your needs.
2. Set the tone controls to 5 or at 12 o'clock and then adjust from there if required.
3. Spend as much time as possible finding a sound you can work with, however don't let it eat into your playing time too much. Sometimes it's the simple things, like having a fresh set of strings or getting your guitar nicely in tune, that can make all the difference.

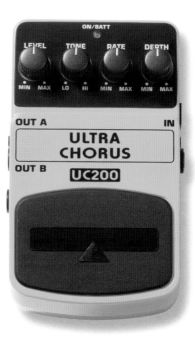

Distortion or Overdrive

This effect can be used to boost an otherwise clean guitar sound to make it sound like the amp is naturally distorting. There are so many types of these pedals available that buying one can be very confusing. Try asking other players what effects they use and why they like them. Also, sometimes these pedals have names that give a few clues as to what type of player they are aimed at, for instance, 'Blues Master Overdrive' or 'Metal God Distortion'.

Chorus/ Flanger or Phaser

These effects can be used to soften up an otherwise plain clean guitar sound. These sounds can make an electric guitar sound almost like an acoustic guitar, and are often used by heavier bands relying on soft intros to maximise the effect of the louder passages. You'll find some great examples of these effects in the earlier Metallica recordings.

Reverb

Reverb is used to emulate the natural reverberation or echo of a large room. This effect, when used at the right settings, can really add a nice dimension to a guitar sound. If used correctly, you'll notice it more when it's not there: it's a great way to naturally 'fatten' up a guitar tone.

Delay

In simple terms, the delay effect can be seen as a repeat effect: it will repeat what you play after you have played it, for as long as you want, depending on how you adjust the delay unit. This effect needs to be approached with great care. If you don't have your settings sorted out, delay can really make a mess out of your sound. First, you will need to adjust the delay time roughly to the song or solo you are playing. Next, you'll need to set the delay to how many repeats and at what level you want those repeats at. Use this effect sparingly at first; if you make a mistake while using it, it repeats the mistake!

Styles of Play

The subject of style is very subjective; there are many factors that will influence your style of electric guitar playing.

There are as many styles of play as there are electric guitar players, so, though it's natural to be drawn to the music you like, it's also a good idea to listen to as many different styles as possible.

Tips:
1. Make a list of songs that you really like and list the things you like about the guitar playing.
2. Try to play along with your favourite songs, and emulate your favourite parts. Making this part of your regular practice routine will lead to some great improvements. If you seem to struggle at first, remember, you are trying to reproduce the best guitar playing that these guitar players could perform at that time.
3. Seek out transcriptions of your favourite guitar music. There are many guitar magazines available at your newsagent that will print between 3 and 5 songs every month.

Playing Standing Up

I suppose it's a reasonable assumption that anyone learning to play the electric guitar has the desire to play with others in a group situation. Most, if not all, guitar players in bands play standing up.

Probably up to this point, you've been doing all your work on your guitar sitting down. Now's the time to start playing the guitar while standing up. You'll need to get a guitar strap and adjust it to the height at which you're most comfortable.

When you first attempt to play standing up, the chances are you will feel very strange. Don't panic; this is perfectly normal.

Try to play the chords that you first learned. You'll need some patience at first, so don't be too hard on yourself. Learning to play standing up is the perfect opportunity to review and consolidate all that you have achieved so far.

Tips:
1. Whenever you play standing up, watch your posture. This is the time to develop good habits; it's natural to want to look at your guitar, but keep a straight – but not stiff – back and avoid slouching over your guitar.
2. You may find that playing the electric guitar standing up is more tiring, so be sure to take short breaks in between practice sessions.
3. Try to watch your favourite guitar players on TV and in concert DVDs. Watch how they perform standing up. Chances are, if they are playing a guitar solo, they will be less active and more focused on their instrument . You'll learn a huge amount just from watching.
4. If you are fortunate enough to have friends that play in a group, whether at a local gig, a rehearsal room or just a garage somewhere, ask if you can go along and watch. Observation will teach you how guitar players make the transition from playing sitting down to playing standing up. You'll also pick up valuable tips about the rehearsal process in a group situation.

Playing With Others

At some stage, while working hard at learning the guitar, you've probably thought about playing with other musicians. The fact that you've decided to make the commitment and learn guitar makes you a musician too, so it's time to find others to jam with. If you already have friends that play, great! If you don't, there are many ways to find others at your level of play to make music with.

Tips:

1. Put an advertisement on the notice board of your local music shop. Make sure you are honest about your level of ability and don't forget to list your favourite bands.

2. Speak to local bands and ask how they made their start. You may be able to pick up invaluable information that will get you moving in the best direction.

3. If you are finding it hard to find others to play with, speak to local music teachers. They are a valuable resource, as they will most certainly have a list of students that will also be looking to play with others.

4. Above all else, try to start playing with a drummer as soon as you can. This way, you'll start to develop a strong sense of timing and rhythm.

5. Whenever possible, always try to play with musicians that are more advanced in playing ability than you. You'll gain encouragement and valuable insight into what you can achieve with some dedication and hard work.

Improvising

The guitar student should start to improvise as soon as possible, both with chords and scales. First of all, let's define what improvising is as it applies to the electric guitar. Improvising is making up music with the music vocabulary that you have been learning. Like learning to speak, the more you learn and practise, the more comfortable you'll feel making up musical ideas.

Improvising is also a great way to improve your guitar playing technique. The most common question I get asked by students is: 'Where and how do I start improvising?' The answer? Anywhere! To start, we'll look at the Pentatonic Minor scale.

Basic Pentatonic Run Through – E minor Pentatonic Ex 1.

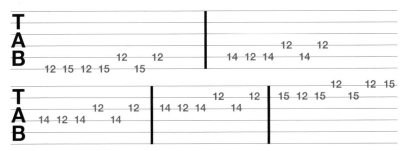

We'll refer to the first 12 bar blues pattern covered in chapter 5. The E minor Pentatonic scale can be matched up with this progression, and can be used to improvise.

E minor Pentatonic Ex 2.

```
T  15p12        12
A     15p12   15p12                15p12         12
B                       14          14p12      14p12
                                                    14

T  14p12        12
A     14p12   14p12                14p12        12
B                       14          14p12      14p12
                                                    15 12
```

1. Review the E Pentatonic shape until you are very familiar with it.
2. Play the first 12 bar progression covered in the More Advanced Chords and Scales chapter a couple of times, and then try the E minor Pentatonic scale with a similar rhythm.

You will find this tough at first, but your efforts will be rewarded! Keep practising, and you'll also find that your ears will start to tune in with what your fingers are trying to do. The more you do this, the better at it you'll get, and the more fun you'll have!

Uncommon Chords

So far in this book we have covered all the standard and essential chord inversions. It would now be a good time to look at some variations and so-called 'uncommon' chords used by guitarists to create a more interesting sound, very similar to how a painter uses different shades and brush strokes on a painting to make it stand out from other paintings.

If you have a look at the chord diagrams for uncommon chords you may notice that in appearance these chords don't seem that different. Once you start playing them, however, you'll notice variations in sound straight away.

Key:
▲ = major, # = sharp, b = flat

Tips:
1. If possible, it would be a great idea to get together with a fellow guitar player and try this approach on other chord progressions.
2. It's also a good idea to mix and match the chord inversions into one guitar part; with this approach, you will be well prepared to put together some excellent guitar parts.

C▲7
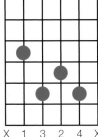
X 1 3 2 4 X

G▲7
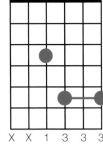
X X 1 3 3 3

G11
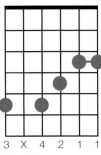
3 X 4 2 1 1

C9
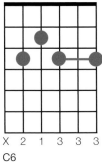
X 2 1 3 3 3

Gadd9
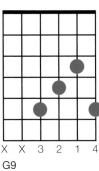
X X 3 2 1 4

C/E
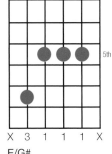
X 3 1 1 1 X   5th

Dsus2
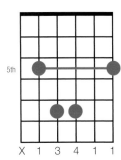
5th
X 1 3 4 1 1

C6
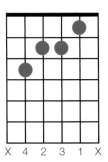
X 4 2 3 1 X

G9
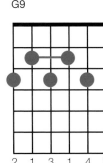
2 1 3 1 4 X

E/G#
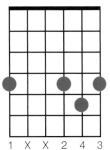
1 X X 2 4 3

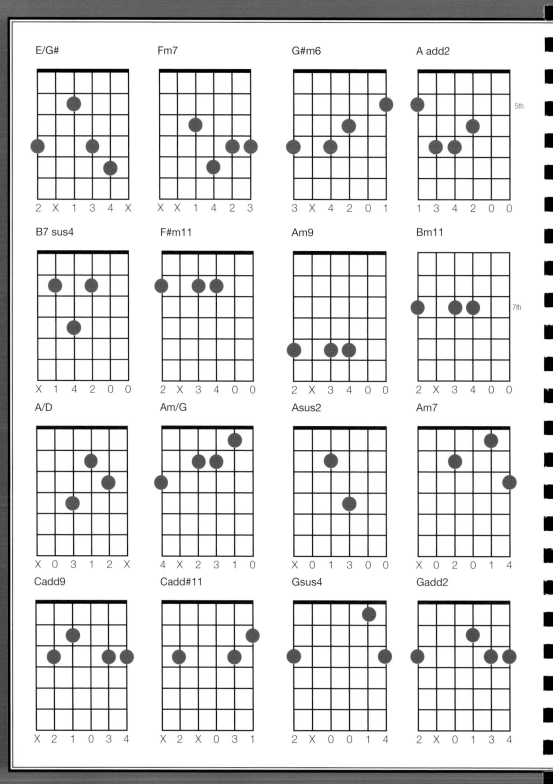

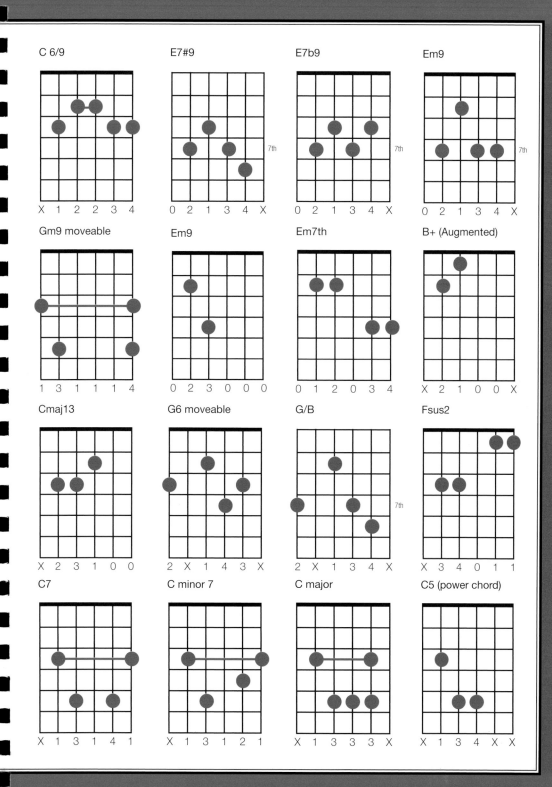

Suggested Practice Schedule

The following example is a suggested practice schedule.

1. 5 minute warm up:
This can include picking up and down and the 3–4 exercise.

2. 15 minutes chord review and chord change exercises:
This should include strumming and rhythm patterns. Use this section of your practice to test your memory and see how many chords you can remember. Make a note of chords that you think need work and could be improved in terms of sound reproduction.

3. 10 minutes scales and scale review:
Practise your scales in different positions (keys) every other practice session. If you do, you will become a lot comfortable playing on most parts of the neck.

4. 10 minutes learning new songs and new techniques:
This can be learning parts of a new song from a guitar magazine. Take your time and be realistic: don't try to learn everything in one hit. Make your goals bite-sized and manageable.

These are, of course, only suggested guidelines. You can change what you practise and how long you work to suit your needs.

It might be a good idea to keep a practice diary or journal. That way, after a few short weeks, you'll get a very clear picture of your guitar playing strengths and where you need to focus more effort.

I'm sure by now, you will have realised, that the guitar is a physical instrument, so I do recommend taking short breaks after your first 15-20 minutes if you need them.

If you are practising sitting down, get up and walk around and do some gentle body stretches before re-commencing.

Conclusion

If you've managed to stay with me up to this point, well done!

Hopefully you've found all of the sections in this book informative and interesting. I've tried to really pack this book with as much practical guitar playing information as possible, but in reality, together, we've just scratched the surface. Having said that, I hope your journey with the electric guitar will be a long and satisfying one.

I think you'll find it a great idea to review the material we've covered here often. I've always found that material I've found challenging today will become very easy later on – if you are prepared to work at it!

In closing, I really want to thank you, the student, for your patience, hard work and sore fingers!

I would like to make some suggestions to help you continue to learn and enjoy the electric guitar.

I cannot stress the importance of finding a really good guitar teacher, especially one as motivated as you are! You may need to try more than one guitar teacher until you find one that you really click with – it's your money, so be fussy!

While there are some great guitar resources on the internet, I would advise using it as sparingly as possible, otherwise you will eat into valuable practice time because of online distractions.

Consider subscribing to a guitar magazine. There are a myriad of publications on the market, so have a look at the ones available at your local newsagent to see what's available and what appeals to you.

Above all, have fun with your electric guitar: keep in mind the music you love and what motivated you to learn the electric guitar.

Simon Croft

About the Author

Simon Croft is an internationally acclaimed guitarist. He was handpicked by Brian May and Roger Taylor from the band Queen to play lead guitar in the Queen/ Ben Elton musical *We Will Rock You*, for which Simon performed over 700 shows; this included a national tour of Australia and two tours of Japan. While in Japan, Simon performed many guitar clinics and was invited by a major music store chain in Tokyo to launch the Brian May model guitar.

Simon has been featured in several guitar publications in Japan, including an interview in the immensely popular magazine *BURRN* and a feature in the *Young Guitar* magazine. Simon has also been featured in the *Australian Guitarist* magazine column "Hot Guitarist". In late 2007, Simon was invited to play lead guitar with Orchestra Victoria in Melbourne, Australia in a show called "Orchestra Victoria Rocks Queen" When told about this show, Brian May from Queen said: "The Bohemian Rhapsody solo couldn't be in better hands".

Simon is an in demand teacher and session player and teaches over 60 students a week. Simon is also a busy live performer and plays over 250 shows a year. A self-confessed guitar tragic, Simon has an extensive personal collection of electric guitars, which include many Fender, Gibson and Gretsch guitar collectables. Simon is endorsed by the internationally renowned company, Ulbrick Guitar Amplifiers and Effects and is personally involved with product improvement and development. Simon's teaching philosophy is simple: "I don't think there is anything more fun or exciting as learning and playing the electric guitar, and I always do my best to make sure the student enjoys the electric guitar as much as I do".

www.simoncroft.com.au